1

1. Introduction

The availability of credit to consumers and businesses is critical to the efficient functioning of the U.S. economy, and finance companies are a key source of such credit. Understanding this industry has been particularly important in the recent financial crisis. Every five years since 1955, the Federal Reserve has undertaken a pair of surveys of the industry—the Census of Finance Companies (CFC) to identify the universe of such companies and to obtain information on general characteristics of those firms and the Survey of Finance Companies (SFC) to obtain more detailed balance-sheet information from a sample of eligible firms identified in the CFC. From the SFC, a sample of firms is selected for a monthly panel survey to provide the timely information on financing needed for policy and research.[1]

In the past, key problems in the CFC/SFC project have been the absence of a comprehensive list of finance companies to serve as the basis of the CFC and the low level of finance company participation. In 2010, these problems were addressed in a major revision of the project in which the survey sampling procedures and instruments were completely redesigned with an eye to improving coverage of the population, increasing response rates, developing systematic means of addressing nonresponse, and reducing reporting errors.

For the purposes of this measurement activity, the target population is the set of domestically operated finance companies. A finance company is defined as any company that holds 50 percent or more of its managed assets in on- or off-balance sheet loans and leases to consumers or businesses and is not chartered as a commercial bank, cooperative bank, credit union, investment bank, savings bank, saving and loan institution, or industrial loan corporation. Partly because the regulation of finance companies is fragmented at the federal and state levels, administrative data are not available to serve as sample frame for finance companies, and comprehensive and specific private data are also unavailable.[2] Therefore, the Federal Reserve developed a procedure for discovering the universe of eligible firms within a list sample frame obtained primarily from Dunn and Bradstreet (D&B) and to a lesser degree from other

---

[1] The data are reported to the public in two monthly statistical releases: *Finance Companies* (G.20) and *Consumer Credit* (G.19), as well as the quarterly *Flow of Funds Accounts of the United States* (Z.1) release. See http://www.federalreserve.gov/econresdata/statisticsdata.htm for more information.

[2] Although finance companies are not subject to federal or state supervision, their practices are regulated by several federal lending statutes, such as Truth in Lending, which for finance companies is enforced by the Federal Trade Commission.

sources. The list was constructed with the intention of being broad enough to include all nondepository companies that provided credit to households or businesses. A questionnaire was mailed to each company in the list.

Although D&B had attempted to filter the main part of the list to include only the highest-level finance company within any given corporate family, responses to the Census quickly revealed that the list contained a complicated tangle of companies, some that were known to be related and others that appeared possibly related. In addition, a substantial number of questionnaires were returned as undeliverable, many were not returned at all, and some were returned with an explicit refusal to participate. Thus, substantial uncertainty remained after the first phase of the CFC about the status of the firms for which a completed questionnaire was not available and about the corporate relationships among companies in both the responding and nonresponding parts of the sample. A nonresponse follow-up study was designed to provide systematic evidence to clarify these issues.

This paper focuses on the use of that follow-up to construct an estimate of the universe that will serve as the basis of the SFC and the development of a simulation method to quantify the uncertainty around the universe estimates. The next section below describes the development of the initial list sample frame for the CFC and the execution of that survey, the following sections present the design and execution of the nonresponse follow-up sample, and the construction of population estimates and associated uncertainty measures. The last section concludes and points to the next stages of the associated work.

2. Developing the initial census frame

Since 1955, the Federal Reserve System has surveyed the assets and liabilities of finance companies at five-year intervals. Through 1975, the universe of all *known* finance companies was surveyed. Since 1980, however, the SFC has been limited to a sample of finance companies selected from the CFC. The 2010 CFC marks a substantial break with the methodology applied in the earlier efforts.[3] In the past, a variety of informal and formal procedures were used to develop a list of finance companies. Although those lists contained all of the largest and best-known finance companies, for a variety of reasons they were unlikely to include less well known small or medium-sized finance

---

[3] The 2000 CFC, a previous version, is described in Dynan *et al.* (2002).

3

companies. For the 2010 Census, an attempt was made to give more comprehensive coverage to the entire range of finance companies.

As noted above, when the CFC was undertaken, no comprehensive and publicly available list of finance companies was available. Dun and Bradstreet (D&B) has a long history of maintaining databases of information on companies operating in the U.S. They use a variety of sources, such as listings in the Yellow Pages, public records of firm transactions, and applications by individual companies to be included in the D&B database. It is generally believed that there is no more comprehensive source of publicly available business lists.[4] To improve the methodology for identifying potential finance companies in the D&B data, we focused on a specific geographic area — the state of Pennsylvania. That state has public records with excellent coverage of finance companies. Using such records obtained from the Pennsylvania Department of Banking (PDB), we identified 2,855 entities that extended credit or were licensed to extend credit and that were not included in the 2005 CFC.[5] In addition, we worked with D&B to study the Standard Industrial Classification (SIC) codes of Pennsylvania companies that were identified in the 2005 CFC either as being finance companies or positively not being finance companies and used that information together with the PDB data to optimize the selection of appropriate SIC codes to be used in generating the frame for the 2010 CFC. Based on the results of this exercise, we determined that inclusion of any of the following three SIC codes in a D&B business record provided the best chance of capturing companies with at least some financing operation:[6]

> 6141 – Non-depository credit institutions - personal credit institutions
>
> 6153 – Non-depository credit institutions - short-term business credit institutions, except agricultural
>
> 6159 – Non-depository credit institutions - miscellaneous business credit institutions[7]

---

[4] The Census Bureau maintains the Longitudinal Business Database (see http://www.census.gov/ces/search.php?search_what=paps&search_terms=LBD&detail_key=101647), which provides information on establishments of firms operating in the U.S. and corporate hierarchy data on those firms. Unfortunately, that information is not available for use outside the Census Bureau or Census Data Centers.

[5] Note that not all of the entities would necessarily qualify as independent finance companies for purposes of the CFC. In the CFC, a case may be out of scope for one of the following reasons: it is a depository, it is not in business, it does not have a sufficient volume of financing relative to its size, or it is the subsidiary of a parent finance company.

[6] D&B records may contain up to six SIC codes.

[7] More details on these codes are available in Appendix A.

SIC codes associated with mortgage lending were not included. A very large number of D&B records contained such codes, and the suspicion was this set included many mortgage brokers, which would not be eligible under the population definition. Because data collected under the Home Mortgage Disclosure Act (HMDA) provide a virtually complete list of mortgage lenders,[8] that information was used to supplement the list derived from D&B data.

Not all D&B records contain information provided directly by the business to which it refers; a variety of other source may have been used. Where SIC codes were inferred from secondary sources, there is a greater possibility that the codes may be in error. Unfortunately, we lacked the information necessary to identify or quantify such errors before the sample selection.

For the set of companies identified using the selected SIC codes, D&B attempted to eliminate finance company subsidiaries of parent firms that were also finance companies under the SIC code classification. About 26,300 companies in the resulting D&B file had at least one of the three target SIC codes. Although the target SIC codes refer to non-depository institutions, about 1,200 records had the words "bank" or "credit union" in their name; we dropped those companies from the list. We dropped another 200 records for various reasons, such as clear evidence of a duplicate record. In all, we retained about 24,800 records from the D&B data. We added about 1,000 additional unique firms from the HMDA data. For a variety of reasons, 833 firms were included in the 2005 CFC data but not the D&B data; these firms were also added. In total, 26,671 records were obtained from the D&B, HMDA or 2005 CFC data. A precise breakdown of the initial sample construction is detailed in Appendix B. Although this initial frame contained many records that appeared quite similar in name and/or shared a common address, we chose to let the responses to the Census help determine the structure of this industry, rather than refine the frame further on an ad hoc basis.

In an attempt to raise the response rate in 2010, we gave respondents the choice to respond on-line or by mail. We redesigned the paper questionnaire to make it more visually appealing and understandable and made the web-based questionnaire as comparable as possible.[9] The online version

---

[8] A nondepository institutions must file mortgage data under HMDA if it meets the following criteria: it is a for-profit institution, its home purchase loan originations exceeded 10 percent of its total loan originations, has a home or branch office in an MSA or received applications for loans or refinancing on property in an MSA, has assets exceeding $10 million or originate 100 or more home purchase loans.
[9] An important influence in this work was Dillman *et al.* (2005).

was a simply designed survey programmed and hosted with the Federal Reserve Bank of Atlanta. For the new paper questionnaire, we worked closely with a graphic designer to incorporate well tested design principles that would make the form clearer and more visually appealing. For example, instructions were placed in close proximity to the corresponding question, and related questions were grouped together in sections surrounded by a black border; rather than use a dense legal-sized format as was done in 2005, the new questionnaire was constructed as a booklet using a smaller page size. The old and new questionnaires are given in Appendix E. We mailed the paper questionnaire to all the firms included in the final list on May 18, 2010 and sent a second mailing five weeks later to firms that had not yet responded, on June 23.

The information collected in the questionnaire was primarily aimed at establishing whether each firm was an eligible finance company and to obtain accurate contact information. Information was also collected on the size (in seven categories) and specialty (business credit, consumer credit, liens on real estate, or no specialty) of each firm, for purposes of establishing a baseline distribution of those characteristics and selecting the sample for the SFC. Completed paper questionnaires were processed using an optical scanning technique.

About 5,700 companies responded to the Census (Table 1) and the on-line option accounted for about one-quarter of the responses. Some of the responses revealed errors in the original sample frame that caused the cases to be out of scope. In total, 4,520 cases were treated as out of scope, primarily because they did not have a sufficient volume of financing relative to the size of their assets or they were not in business. A substantial part of the sample, about 6,400 cases, did not have an opportunity to respond, because the questionnaire mailed to them was returned by the post office as undeliverable.[10] In addition, we detected larger patterns of corporate relationships among firms after examining the records received. Among the nonrespondents, numerous groups of records had similar company names. Records with similar names could be subsidiaries of the same company, independent franchises of the same company, duplicates of one another, or possibly unrelated.

---

[10] In processing the responses, it was determined that 12 parent finance companies of subsidiaries responding to the Census had not been included in the original list sample; these observations were added to the sample and treated as nonrespondents. The reference to the parent company in the data provided by the subsidiaries serves to give a type of representation for the parent in the main sample, though technically the cases are an example of frame error.

3. Designing a follow-up survey with nonrespondents

After the two waves of mailings, little or nothing was known about more than three-quarters of the original list sample. If the responses received were simply a random sample of the full list sample ("missing completely at random" or MCAR) or were a random sample conditional upon a set of characteristics observable for all cases ("missing at random" or MAR), then it would be a straightforward matter to weight the set of respondents to represent the set of all finance companies. Unfortunately, we have no information to suggest that assuming such a simple pattern of nonresponse is appropriate. Furthermore, good survey practice and official OMB guidance for surveys require an analysis to explore potential nonresponse biases when response rates are so low.[11]

To gain a better understanding of the nature of nonresponse in the CFC and the effects of nonresponse on population estimates from the data, we designed and undertook a follow-up survey with cases that did not respond to the CFC, including cases for which the questionnaire was returned as being undeliverable. External considerations imposed a limit of about 3,000 observations that could be pursued in the follow-up study. Particular objectives of the follow-up study were to characterize the unobserved population as in or out of scope, and if in scope, to estimate the distribution of the characteristics of the unobserved in-scope companies.

As noted above, close examination of the responses in the first stage of the CFC revealed that the procedure applied by D&B to remove subsidiaries of parent finance companies was not fully successful. In light of this finding, we examined the nonrespondent records and found patterns in name and address data that strongly suggested similar clustering among those records. Thus, a special focus was needed in the follow-up to gain information on the extent of such problems among the unobserved population. We determined that we could more efficiently characterize the degree of clustering if we could create candidate clusters and examine several companies within each such cluster. For this reason, we decided to organize the follow-up study in two major parts: one part focused on a sample of observations that could be placed in candidate cluster arrangements, and the other part focused on the remaining cases.

---

[11] See http://www.whitehouse.gov/sites/default/files/omb/assets/omb/inforeg/statpolicy/ standards_stat_surveys.pdf .

To develop plausible clusters of records, we began by standardizing common words in company names. For example, "association" became "assn," and "corporation" became "corp." Then we clustered records according to a set of criteria based on the similarity of their names (Appendix C). Although such clusters would miss groups of related companies that happen to have very different names, such companies would, in principle, be captured in the sample of unclustered cases. We targeted selecting 25 percent of the follow-up sample (750 records) from the clustered records and the remaining 75 percent from the non-clustered records; these fractions are approximately the proportions of such cases in the full set of cases available for sampling for the follow-up.

The number of each firm's employees, as reported in the D&B data, played a key role in the design of the follow-up sample. This measure was available for more than 90 percent of the relevant records and was believed to be reasonably reliable; the value was missing for a relatively small number of cases derived from either the 2005 CFC or the HMDA data.[12] We devised the following plan for imputing this value for all cases (respondents and nonrespondents) for which it was missing. Where the value was not available, but the asset size category of a company was reported on the CFC, we assigned the median number of employees for firms within the relevant asset size category, using data from the companies that responded to the CFC (Table 2). If both the number of employees and the asset size category were missing, we estimated the company's asset size category in one of two ways. For the 516 companies that did not have the employee size or asset size available but had responded to the 2005 CFC, we first used the 2005 asset size category as a proxy for the 2010 asset size category and then imputed the employee count using this asset size to condition the imputation. For each of the 509 companies that were taken from the HMDA data and, thus, had neither employee size or asset size data available, we estimated its asset size category using the relationship between asset size category and mortgage originations among the firms that responded to the CFC. As shown in Table 3, we calculated the median mortgage origination for each asset size category for the HMDA respondents, and that value was used as the upper bound of the range of mortgage originations corresponding to each asset size category. After imputing the asset size category for these companies, we imputed the employee count using the same procedure as when the asset category was known. Although the use of the median to anchor the ranges

---

[12] Many other candidate variables were considered, but were ruled out by virtue of high rates of missing data or questions about reliability for the purpose.

may ultimately introduce some bias in the estimates of employee counts, this approach is a reasonably robust way of dealing with outliers in the range of mortgage originations within asset classes.

For the clustered part of the sample, we chose to select cases in two stages. At the first stage, we selected clusters with probability proportional to the total number of employees of all the firms in the cluster. The distribution of clusters by total employee count is significantly right-skewed, with a mean of 842 employees and a median of 8 employees (Figure 1). We sampled with probability one those clusters whose total number of employees was in the top 5 percent (112 employees). These "certainty" clusters accounted for 114 clusters of the 2,265 clusters we identified. We sampled the remaining "non-certainty" clusters using probability-proportional-to-size (PPS) sampling without replacement. We stratified the total cluster population into 3 groups according to the cumulative square root f rule (Dalenius and Hodges, 1959), based on the number of records in the cluster. Given this stratification of clusters, the probability of selecting non-certainty cluster j in stratum h becomes k_h/K_h, where k_h is the number of sampled clusters that contain nonrespondents and K_h the number of clusters in the stratum h that contain nonrespondents. Using this method, we chose 256 clusters, or 11.3 percent of the clusters we identified. In total, we chose 370 clusters for the follow-up survey.

At the second stage, we sampled companies from each of the chosen clusters. In order to evaluate the true extent of relationships within clusters, we determined that it would be sufficient to select a random subsample of two records for clusters containing fewer than 6 firms, three records for clusters containing between 6 and 10 firms, and 4 records for clusters containing more than 10 firms. In order to assess the relationship among all firms, the clusters were designed to include all nonrespondents as well as responding firms potentially associated with the nonrespondent firms, according to our clustering rules. If a randomly sampled company was a nonrespondent, it was included in the follow-up sample. Companies selected that were nonrespondents at the first stage were added to the follow-up sample; companies selected that had been respondents at the first stage were not added to the follow-up sample, but were used only in characterizing the relationship among firms in the cluster. Nonrespondent records chosen from both the "certainty" and "noncertainty" clusters totaled 628, or about 21 percent of the total nonresponse sample, somewhat less than our target of 25 percent.[13] Define

$$Z_i = \begin{cases} 1 & \text{if unit } i \text{ is in the follow-up sample} \\ 0 & \text{otherwise} \end{cases}$$

(1)

Then the probability of including the ith nonresponding company in the sample is:

$$\pi_i = P(Z_i = 1) = \frac{m_c}{M_c}$$

(2)

where M_c is the number of nonrespondent companies in a cluster and m_c is the number of companies randomly chosen from that cluster that did not respond to the Census.

We chose the remaining 79 percent of the follow-up sample from the set of non-clustered nonrespondent records, also stratified by the total number of employees. The distribution of employees among the non-clustered, nonrespondent records is also significantly right-skewed, but with a smaller average number of employees than among firms in the clusters (Figure 2). We sampled with certainty the 701 firms with a total number of employees in the top 5 percent of the non-clustered firms (about 30 employees). In addition, D&B data for 111 nonresponding companies indicated that their total number of employees was zero; other data for these cases suggested that this value might be erroneous. To insure against distortions induced by such cases, we included all of them in the sample with certainty. Altogether, records sampled with certainty accounted for 812 records—5.6 percent—of all the non-clustered nonrespondents.

We stratified the remaining population into three mutually exclusive employee-size groups by using the cumulative square root f rule. We sampled these records in proportion to the number of nonresponses in each of the three size categories. Taking m_s as the number of sampled units in each stratum and M_s as the total number of units in stratum s, the probability of an individual unit being

---

[13] For twelve clusters, all of the companies chosen for the follow-up had responded to the survey, while other companies in the cluster had not responded. To account for the nonrespondents in these clusters, we added one pseudo-observation to the sample from each of these clusters; the analysis weights for these pseudo-observations are taken to represent the nonrespondents in these clusters.

selected in the follow-up sample is m_s/M_s. In total from the non-clustered cases, we chose 1,545 non-certainty nonrespondents.

Using the notation developed above, the probability of inclusion in the nonresponse follow-up sample can be summarized as:

$$\alpha_i = \begin{cases} \pi_i & i \in \text{certainty cluster} \\ \dfrac{k_h}{K_h}\pi_i & i \in \text{non-certainty cluster, } h=1,2,3 \\ 1 & i \in \text{non-clustered certainty strata or 15 identified but nonresponding parent companies} \\ \dfrac{m_s}{M_s} & i \in \text{non-clustered non-certainty strata, } s=1,2,3 \end{cases} \tag{3}$$

Among the clustered records, the sample was heavily concentrated on the clusters with between 2 and 5 observations, for both the certainty and non-certainty parts of that subsample (Table 4). The median number of employees for companies within the chosen clustered records was small—only 3 employees. Similarly, the majority of the non-clustered companies selected were relatively small as well— a median of 3 employees.

4. Conducting the nonresponse follow-up

The field work for the nonresponse follow-up was conducted in August and September of 2010 by analysts in the statistics staff at all twelve Federal Reserve Banks. Each Reserve Bank was randomly assigned between 200 and 300 companies. The immediate objectives of the follow-up were the same as those of the initial survey: to determine whether each company in the follow-up sample met the definition of a finance company, to obtain accurate contact information, and to learn about the size and specialty of the company. The larger objective of the follow-up was to determine how similar or dissimilar the nonrespondents to the CFC were from the group that responded, and to incorporate that information in our estimates of the overall size of the universe of finance companies and the distribution of companies by size and specialties.

Analysts attempted to contact each company in the sample, using the contact information in the initial record. If the analyst successfully contacted the company, the analyst attempted to collect information directly from the company over the telephone. In case the respondent was willing to answer only a few questions, the analyst began with the most crucial information for determining whether a company met the definition of a finance company. If she was unsuccessful in collecting this information at that point, she requested the company to answer the remaining questions from the CFC, preferably online in order to control costs. If the company declined to provide any information, the analyst conducted a search on the company, using a variety of resources on the Internet. Because many company names in the follow-up were similar, analysts searched for the exact company name, along with the city and state where the company was located. If no company by that name was found, analysts expanded their search to nearby cities. Analysts searched for a confirmation that the company existed, whether it appeared to make loans or leases and of what kind (consumer, real estate, business), an indication of the type of business (cash advance, mortgage company, auto dealer, etc.), and an indication of the size of the company (number of offices, asset size, number of employees, etc.).

If the analyst was unable to contact the company successfully using the information in the initial record, she searched for new contact information. With this new information, the analyst again attempted to contact the company. If successful, the analyst proceeded as above. If unsuccessful, the analyst initiated research as in the case of companies that declined to participate.

5. Analysis of follow-up responses

We categorized responses to the follow-up to aid in the estimation of the universe. We first grouped the initial follow-up sample into companies that were known not to exist, those with which we made some sort of contact but whose existence as an on-going concern was unknown, and those that were known for certain to exist as a finance company (Figure 3). For present purposes, we take nonexistent companies as consisting of two types: companies that were out of business or going out of business (confirmed through various channels, such as websites, current employees, or other people contacted by the analyst) and companies that we were unable to contact or locate in any way; given the intensity of the search the analysts made for firms, it appears nearly certain that companies in the latter subset were out

12

of business.[14] We categorized a company into the "some contact" group if the analyst reached voice mail that identified the company, but no other contact was made. For companies known to exist as an on-going business of any sort, we created a subclassification depending on whether or not we obtained sufficient information to determine whether the firm was out of scope based on the percentage of their business in loans or leases.

Among companies for which we had such loan or lease information, 502 of them were in the non-clustered part of the nonresponse follow-up sample and 112 were in the clustered part. For the non-clustered companies, we discovered that 139 of the companies were independent finance companies (that is, not the subsidiary of another company), 44 were related to another company, 26 finance companies had unknown corporate structure and the remaining 293 companies did not have sufficient loan operations to qualify as finance companies. For the clustered companies, 28 were determined to be independent finance companies, 39 were related to another company, 1 company had unknown status and the remaining 44 companies were not considered as finance companies.

6. Calculation of analysis weights

The categories described in the section above and in Figure 3 form the broad basis for our estimate of the universe. In order that a variety of estimates could be calculated from these data,[15] we created analysis weights for companies included in the follow-up sample to represent the nonrespondents at the first stage. Combining those weighted observations and the first-stage observations (which have a weight of one) we can produce estimates for the entire universe. An alternative to weighting would be to develop a unique estimator for each statistic of interest; however, we did not pursue that option due to limited resources and the desire that these data be easily usable in a variety of ways.

The weights for the follow-up respondents were constructed in several stages. We begin with a base weight that reflects a company's inclusion in the follow-up sample. The base weight, shown in equation 4, is the inverse of the probability that it was included in this sample (see equation 3).

---

[14] We defined a case as a noncontact in the follow-up if no phone number was available, the phone number was nonworking, the phone was unanswered and no voice mail available, or the person who answered the phone was not connected with the company.

[15] The construction of analysis weights depends on the observed information. For that reason, careful attention was required to maximize the reliability of the data. Data editing is discussed in Appendix E and item nonresponse imputation in Appendix F.

$$w_i^B = \frac{1}{\alpha_i}$$

$$(4)$$

We then went through a multi-stage process to adjust this weight so that each follow-up respondent's weight accounts for its directly estimated share in the population as well as the share of the nonrespondents to the follow-up that we judge to be most like it. To address the representation of the nonrespondents, we adjusted the base weight of respondents to account for the probability that some of the nonrespondents to the follow-up were in existence, had at least 50 percent of its assets in loans or leases, and was an independent company. This probability can be decomposed into three parts: first, the probability that a company exists; second, the probability that it meets the appropriate definition of a finance company, given that it exists; and third, the probability that the company is an independent company, given that it is an existing finance company. We specify estimates of each these probabilities and corresponding adjustments to the weights in turn below.

The first part is the likelihood that the company exists. From the follow-up, it is known that there were 588 entities with which there was some contact, but whose existence status was not determined definitively; the weighted fraction of such cases is given by n_S/n. The data do not allow us to say precisely what fraction of all firms unobserved in the CFC exist, but they do allow us to bound an estimate. The lower bound of the probability that a firm exists is the weighted proportion of the entire follow-up sample that is known to exist (n_E/n) and the upper bound is one minus the weighted proportion of that sample that is known not to exist (n_N/n) (equation 5),

$$f_E \in \left[\frac{n_E}{n}, 1 - \frac{n_N}{n} \right] = \left[\frac{n_E}{n}, \frac{(n_E + n_S)}{n} \right]$$

$$(5)$$

where the n's are defined as:

$$n_x = \sum_{i=1}^{n} w_i^B n_{xi}$$

$$(6)$$

14

where n_{xi} is an indicator variable that takes on the value of 1 if company i is in group x and n is the number of observations in the follow-up sample.

For the main weight, we averaged the lower and upper bounds, which is equivalent to assuming that half the original nonrespondents with whom we had some contact in the follow-up actually exist. We further refined this estimate by calculating it for C different classes of companies within the follow-up sample, so that it applies to respondents with similar characteristics. For class c, the probability of existence becomes $\hat{f}_E^c$ (equation 7). We estimated the probability of existence separately conditional on postal return status, clustering status, employee size and cluster size (Table 5).

$$\hat{f}_E^c = \frac{1}{2}\left[\frac{n_E^c}{n^c} + \frac{\left(n_E^c + n_S^c\right)}{n^c}\right] = \frac{n_E^c}{n^c} + \frac{n_S^c}{2n^c} \tag{7}$$

With this probability we can calculate the relevant adjustment to the analysis weights. Intuitively, each company in the follow-up sample that actually exists must not only represent itself, but also must represent companies with which we had only some contact, but whom we assumed were in existence. We calculated the adjustment by dividing the total number of companies assumed to exist in the follow-up sample ($n^c f_E^c$, where n^c is the weighted number of companies in class c of the follow-up sample, and f_E^c is the probability of existence for class c) equally among the companies that actually exist (n_E^c) (equation 8).

$$q_E^c = \frac{n^c \hat{f}_E^c}{n_E^c} = 1 + \frac{n_S^c}{2n_E^c} \tag{8}$$

The second probability estimated is the likelihood that the company meets the definition of a finance company, given that it exists. At issue here are companies known to exist but for which we do not have information on the percentage of their total gross assets in loans or leases. Similar to the estimate of existence above, in theory we can set the lower bound of the probability that a firm is a finance company as the weighted proportion of existing companies whose gross loans and leases are 50 percent or more of total assets, and the upper bound as one minus the proportion of existing companies whose gross loans and leases are less than 50 percent of total assets. In the fully observed data, approximately 42 percent of non-clustered respondents and 60 percent of clustered respondents to the follow-up who are currently in business met this part of the definition of a finance company, which argues against our averaging the upper and lower bounds. Therefore in practice, we set this probability equal to the weighted share of respondents to the follow-up currently in business who met the definition of a finance company. The weighting procedure is defined as follows:

$$n_x = \sum_{i=1}^{n} w_i^B q_{Ei} n_{xi}$$

(9)

where n_{xi} is an indicator variable that takes on the value of 1 if company i is in group x. The indicator variable is now weighted by the product of the base weight and the weight-adjustment factor for existence from the previous stage. We can also refine this estimate further by calculating it for D different classes, so that probability of being a finance company for a company in class d becomes $\hat{f}_{F|E}^d$ (equation 10), where n_{EF}^d is the weighted number of existing companies that are known to be finance companies and n_{EK}^d is the weighted number of existing companies for which the loan share is known. After some experimentation, we created classes based on clustering status and employee size and collapsed cells when data were sparse (Table 6).

$$\hat{f}_{F|E}^d = \frac{n_{EF}^d}{n_{EK}^d}$$

(10)

To adjust the weights of existing companies that qualify as finance companies so that they also represent existing finance companies for whom we have no loan information, we calculate the number of existing companies that we assume to be finance companies (where n_{EU}^d is the weighted share of companies for which loan share is unknown) and divide them equally among existing companies that are known to be finance companies (equation 11).

16

$$q^d_{F|E} = \frac{n^d_{EF} + n^d_{EU}\hat{f}^d_{F|E}}{n^d_{EF}} = 1 + \frac{n^d_{EU}}{n^d_{EK}} \tag{11}$$

The final probability required is the likelihood that a company is independent, rather than a subsidiary of another company, given that it exists and is a finance company. We set this probability equal to the weighted share of independent finance companies among finance companies with known corporate structure information. The weighting procedure is as follows:

$$n_x = \sum_{i=1}^{n} w_i^B q_{Ei} q_{F|Ei} n_{xi} \tag{12}$$

This estimate is further refined by calculating it for the same D different classes as the previous stage, so that probability of being an independent finance company for a company in class d becomes $\hat{f}^d_{I|FE}$ (equation 13).

$$\hat{f}^d_{I|FE} = \frac{n^d_{EFI}}{n^d_{EFK}} \tag{13}$$

Where n^d_{EFI} is the weighted number of existing finance companies that are known to be independent and n^d_{EFK} is the weighted number of existing finance companies for which corporate structure is known. The weight adjustment factor for this stage is to increase weights of independent finance companies (n_{EFI}) to compensate for finance companies with unknown corporate structure information (n^d_{EFU}) (equation 14). Again, it is computed separately for each of the D classes.

$$q^d_{I|FE} = \frac{n^d_{EFI} + n^d_{EFU}\hat{f}_{I|FE}}{n^d_{EFI}} = 1 + \frac{n^d_{EFU}}{n^d_{EFK}} \tag{14}$$

For clustered companies, an additional adjustment to the base weight is necessary. If companies in a cluster are indeed all related to each other through a subsidiary-parent relationship, then there is only one independent finance company in the cluster. If the companies in a cluster are not related, then the companies in the cluster must be treated as if they were independent companies. To accomplish this, we estimated the probability that the companies in a given cluster are indeed related to each other, setting this probability equal to the weighted share of related clusters (k_R) among sampled clusters with known relationship (equation 15). We estimated this probability to be 0.66. Clusters that are not related are denoted as k_N. The weights used were the inverse of the probability that the cluster was selected for the nonresponse follow-up.

$$\hat{f}_R = \frac{k_R}{k_R + k_N}$$

(15)

The weight adjustment factor increases weights of not related clusters (k_N) to represent clusters with unknown relationship (k_U) but are likely to be not related (equation 16).

$$q_N = \frac{k_N + k_U\left(1 - \hat{f}_R\right)}{k_N} = 1 + \frac{k_U}{k_R + k_N}$$

(16)

Similarly, the weight adjustment factor here is to increase weights of related clusters so that they also represent clusters with unknown relationship but are likely to be related (equation 17).

$$q_R = \frac{k_R + k_U\hat{f}_R}{k_R} = 1 + \frac{k_U}{k_R + k_N}$$

(17)

The weights for related companies in a cluster need an additional adjustment. Their weights must be adjusted downwards so that the entire cluster represents only one independent finance company. This downward adjustment is the inverse of π_i, which can be thought of as the number of companies in the nonresponse population represented by the sampled company. The final weight assigned to a company is:

18

$$
w_i = \begin{cases} w_i^B q_{Ei} q_{F|Ei} q_{I|FEi}, & \text{for non-clustered sample} \\ w_i^B q_{Ei} q_{F|Ei} q_{I|FEi} q_R \pi_i, & \text{for clustered but related sample} \\ w_i^B q_{Ei} q_{F|Ei} q_{I|FEi} q_N, & \text{for clustered but not related sample} \end{cases} \tag{18}
$$

We use these final weights to estimate the number of existing, independent finance companies within the entire nonrespondent universe.

7. Description of universe estimate

To estimate the number of finance companies, we assigned a weight of one to the respondents to the CFC that were independent finance companies, and we assigned the appropriate analysis weight described in equation 18 to follow-up respondents that were independent finance companies. In all, our estimate of the number of finance companies in the United States is a bit over 5,000 (Table 7). A large proportion of the estimated set of finance companies consisted of firms with 10 or fewer employees. The majority of these small companies appear to have been consumer lenders (Table 8).

7.1. Examination of nonresponse bias using the nonresponse follow-up

One way to gauge the value of the nonresponse follow-up is to estimate the number of finance companies in the United States, assuming the CFC nonresponse was random within adjustment classes. This assumption is one we could make if no additional information about the nonrespondents had been collected through the follow-up effort. Under this assumption, we would estimate about 8,700 finance companies, or 60 percent more companies than we estimated using the follow-up respondents and their computed analysis weights (Table 7, column 1). The assumption that nonresponse is random seems to be most inappropriate for the two smallest employee size categories. For example, the number of firms estimated in the 1 - 3 employee size category is more than twice as high under the random nonresponse assumption than using the follow-up. This implies that the firms in the nonresponse follow-up for this group were less likely to be finance companies than the firms who responded to the CFC in the first stage. In contrast, for firms with 30 or more employees, the firms in the nonresponse follow-up were more likely to be finance companies than the firms who responded to the CFC in the first stage. Thus, the number of companies in this size group is larger when we use the follow-up respondents and appropriate weights than when we assume random nonresponse.

7.2. Variance estimation

Because it was not possible to pursue or interview every nonrespondent to the first stage of the CFC and because information was not obtained for all cases in that sample, there is inherent uncertainty about the size and distribution of characteristics of the true universe of finance companies. An important source of the variability of our outcome measures is a consequence of sampling in the follow-up survey, and in principle, there are well defined approaches for estimating associated variances. However, there is also potential for variability in the assumptions necessary at the various stages of weight adjustment. In the discussion that follows, we have attempted to allow for variability of those assumptions within ranges we believe are plausible, but others might have different views. Consequently, the estimates of variability presented here should only be taken as indicative of the true level of uncertainty in our estimates.

The complexity of the design for the nonresponse follow-up sample for the CFC and the potential for variability in the assumptions used in calculating the universe estimates preclude use of a standard analytical approximation of the distribution of sampling error; instead, we used a replication method to estimate the variance associated with our estimates of the finance company universe. We used a bootstrap technique, which allows direct evaluation of the sampling distribution of the estimates and derivation of the confidence intervals for the universe estimates. We started with 1,000 replicate sets of the full nonresponse sample according to the rules defined below. All the observations that belonged to either the certainty clusters or the non-clustered certainty group were automatically included in each replicate exactly once. Following the design of the follow-up sample, clusters from the follow-up were randomly selected with replacement, from the pool of non-certainty clusters that were included in the nonresponse follow-up. Once a cluster was selected, every observation in that cluster was included in the replicate set. All the sample observations that were part of the non-clustered non-certainty groups were pooled together by strata, and were randomly sampled with replacement.

As shown in equations 5-17, we made various assumptions at each stage of estimation, with only limited knowledge of the true nature of the underlying distributions of outcomes. To give an indication of error associated with this incomplete information, we placed a crude prior distribution on each of the ranges of adjustment factors and used those distributions together with the bootstrap replicates to calculate a broader measure of the distribution of estimation error. For each proportion used in the stages of weight adjustment, we assumed a discrete distribution with 60 percent of the mass on the baseline estimated proportions and 20 percent each on deviations 10 percentage points above and below that proportion. For example, three times in five, 50 percent of the companies with unknown existence status were considered to have been in existence, one time in five 40 percent were considered to have been in existence, and one time in five 60 percent were considered to have been in existence. By interacting the outcomes from each of the distributions at each of the four adjustment stages, we had 625 scenarios. Computing the results of each scenario using data from the 1,000 replicate sets yielded 625,000 estimates.[16]

For each such estimate, we created the appropriate replicate weights and computed the point estimate. Confidence intervals and standard errors for the universe estimates were constructed and results are displayed in Table 8. For example, we estimate that there were 2,339 firms with less than $1 million in assets and the standard error of that estimate is 179—for a coefficient of variation of 0.077. Largely because there is so much information publicly available about the largest firms—those with more than $20 billion in asset—variability of our estimate of the size of that group appears negligible.

8. Conclusion

In 2010, the Census of Finance Companies underwent a major revision that addressed both the absence of a comprehensive list of finance companies to serve as the basis of the CFC and low survey response rates in previous waves. Initial responses to the CFC revealed that the sample frame contained a complex tangle of often interrelated companies, which had not been expected from the description of the frame used to identify the universe of finance companies. Moreover, nonresponse remained substantial in the 2010 CFC. Both the interrelationship of companies and complicated patterns of nonresponse across groups indicated that nonrespondents were not missing at random. Thus, we undertook a large-scale follow-up study to characterize the patterns of nonresponse and relationship.

---

[16] Because the central point in the prior distributions is repeated three times, the actual number of calculations necessary was reduced to 81,000.

To address the complexity of the relationships among firms in the sample frame, we organized the follow-up study by splitting the sample into two major parts: one part focused on a sample of observations in candidate cluster arrangements, and the other part focused on the remaining unclustered cases. Results of the follow-up survey indicate that the size of the universe of finance companies was smaller than would have been estimated from the original respondents, assuming that missing observations were distributed in the same way as the respondents, a difference largely accounted for by a relatively high rate of response among small finance companies.

The estimates for the CFC are affected both by sampling at the stage of the follow-up sample and by potential variation in the assumptions necessary to extrapolate the results of follow-up study to the universe. To that end, we used a combination of a bootstrap procedure intended to account for sampling and a set of prior distributions placed on the assumptions in order to simulate the range of estimation error.

The results of the CFC will be used along with detailed balance sheet data obtained from a sample of the CFC respondents in the Survey of Finance Companies to create benchmark estimates of credit provided by finance companies to consumers and businesses. That information in turn will be used to support higher-frequency estimates of such credit from a monthly panel of finance companies.

References

Dalenius, T. and Hodges, J. L. (1959) Minimum Variance Stratification. *Journal of the American Statistical Association*, 54, 88-101.

Dillman, D., Gertseva, A. and Mahon-Haft, T. (2005) Achieving Usability in Establishment Surveys Through the Application of Visual Design Principles. *Journal of Official Statistics*, Vol. 21, No. 2, pp. 183-214.

Dynan, Karen E., Johnson, Katheen W. and Slowinski, Samuel M. (2002) Survey of Finance Companies, 2000. *Federal Reserve Bulletin*, vol. 88, pp. 1-14.

Rubin, D.B. (1987) *Multiple Imputation for Nonresponse in Surveys*. J. Wiley & Sons, New York.

Table 1: Response to 2010 CFC[17]

Disposition	Wave 1	Wave 2	Total
Total mailed	26,671	19,998	NA
Any mode of response	3,545	2,187	5,732
by paper	2,672	1,690	4,362
by web	873	497	1,370
Nonrespondent	17,975	14,491	14,491
Postal return	5,151	1,297	6,448
Final case disposition			
In scope cases and completed	1,407	638	2,045
Out of scope	2,241	2,279	4,520
Not in business	602	526	1,128
Insufficient loan/lease operation	1,147	769	1,916
Bank or bank holding company	112	63	175
Bank subsidiary	39	15	54
Finance company subsidiary or branch	144	124	268
Excluded[18]	197	782	979
Unable to determine whether in scope	3	3	6

---

[17] Includes responses received as of July 29th, 2010 prior to the nonresponse follow-up sample selection.

[18] Excluded cases include companies that are part of the Farm Credit System, affiliated with a cooperative, identified as subsidiaries of a parent company, companies determined to be the same company based on identical name and nearly identical address, or for other miscellaneous reasons. These reflect later review and revisions to the data.

Table 2: Median number of employees, by asset category

Asset size category	Number of D&B Census respondents with non-missing employee data	Median number of employees for the D&B respondents	Number of records with imputed employee count
Less than $1 million	2,128	3	382
$1 - $10 million	894	4	529
$10 - $100 million	448	10	444
$100 million - $1 billion	216	32	257
$1 billion – $3 billion	66	52	25
$3 billion - $20 billion	52	180	23
Greater than $20 billion	29	11,900	15
Total	3,833	3	1,675

Table 3: Median mortgage originations, by asset category

Asset size category	Number of HMDA Census respondents	Median mortgage loan origination for the HMDA respondents	Mortgage originations	Number of records with imputed asset data
Less than $1 million	67	$21.6 million	< $22 million	112
$1 – 10 million	125	$89.4 million	$22 - $90 million	161
$10 - $100 million	112	$295.7 million	$90 - $300 million	149
$100 million - $1 billion	NA	NA	> $300 million	87
Total	304	NA	NA	509

Table 4: Source of nonresponse follow-up records[19]

	Total obs. (number)	Non-respondents (number)	Non-respondent share of total obs. (percent)	Chosen for Non-response follow-up (number)	Percent of non-respondents chosen for follow-up (Percent)
Clustered records	6,873	5,629	83	628	11
Certainty clusters	804	655	81	186	28
2 – 5 obs.	219	132	60	104	79
6 – 10 obs	68	52	76	20	38
More than 10 obs.	517	471	91	62	13
Noncertainty clusters	6,069	4,974	82	442	9
2 – 5 obs.	4,798	3,831	80	336	9
6 – 10 obs.	774	687	99	51	7
More than 10 obs.	497	456	92	55	12
Non-clustered records	18,889	14,488	77	2,357	16
No employees	142	111	78	111	100
1-3 employees	12,425	10,108	81	1,143	11
4-10 employees	4,162	2,884	69	325	11
11 – 29 employees	1,030	684	66	77	11
More than 29 employees	1,130	701	62	701	100
Subtotal	25,762	20,117	78	2,985	15
Identified parent companies	19	15	79	15	100
Excluded[20]	902	819	91	0	0
Total	26,683	20,951	79	3,000	14

---

[19] Data are as of July 29th, 2010 prior to the nonresponse follow-up sample selection.
[20] Excluded cases include companies that are part of the Farm Credit System, affiliated with a cooperative, identified as subsidiaries of a parent company, and companies determined to be the same company based on identical name and nearly identical address.

Table 5: The probability of existence ($\hat{f}_E^c$), by class

Postal return status	Non-clustered, by number of employees					Clustered, by number of observations in the cluster		
	No employees	1-3 employees	4-10 employees	11-29 employees	More than 29 employees	2-5 obs	6-10 obs	More than 10 obs
No	0.53	0.50	0.62	0.56	0.66	0.69	0.83	0.73
Yes	0.38	0.25	0.27	0.25	0.42	0.37	0.39	0.44

Table 6: The probability of being a finance company conditional on existence ($\hat{f}_{EF}^d$), by class

Non-clustered			Clustered
Less than 4 employees	4-29 employees	More than 29 employees	
0.41	0.39	0.47	0.60

Table 7: Estimate of the finance company universe under various treatment of nonresponse, by employee size

Employee size category	Without follow-up: nonresponse assumed to be MAR* (1)	With follow-up: using results of the follow-up study (2)
No employees	45	14
1-3 employees	5,028	2,458
4-10 employees	2,445	1,815
11-29 employees	602	321
More than 29 employees	652	738
Total	8,772	5,346

*Missing at random.

Table 8: Estimate of the finance company universe by employee size and loan specialty

Employee size category	Loan specialty category		
	Business	Consumer	Other
No employees	8	6	1
1-3 employees	432	1,646	379
4-10 employees	313	1,099	404
11-29 employees	163	122	36
More than 29 employees	224	184	329
Total	1,140	3,057	1,149

Table 9: Estimate of the finance company universe, 95% bootstrap percentile confidence interval and standard error, by asset size

Asset size category	Estimate	Lower limit	Upper limit	Standard error
Less than $1 million	2,339	1,779	2,478	179
$1 - $10 million	1,348	1,093	1,580	125
$10 - $100 million	1,261	1,088	1,880	200
$100 million - $1 billion	290	210	455	64
$1- $3 billion	63	44	97	16
$3 - $20 billion	25	24	26	1
Greater than $20 billion	20	20	21	0
Total	5,346	4,670	6,007	340

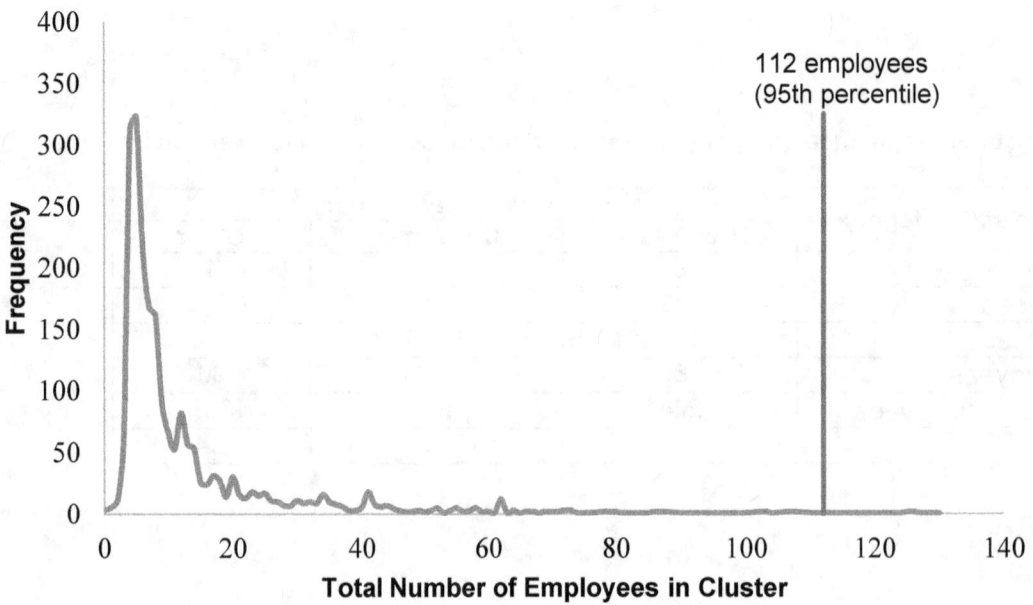

Note: Clusters with more than 130 emplyees are not included in this chart.

Figure 1: Frequency distribution of clusters by total number of employees

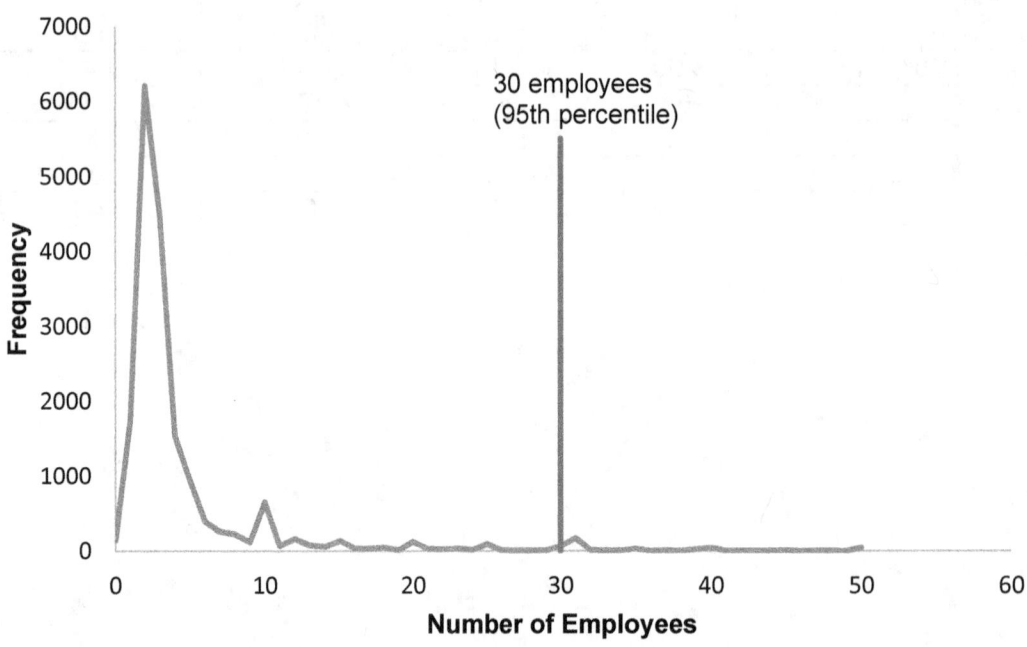

Note: Companies with more than 50 employees are not included in this chart.

Figure 2: Frequency distribution of employees for non-clustered companies

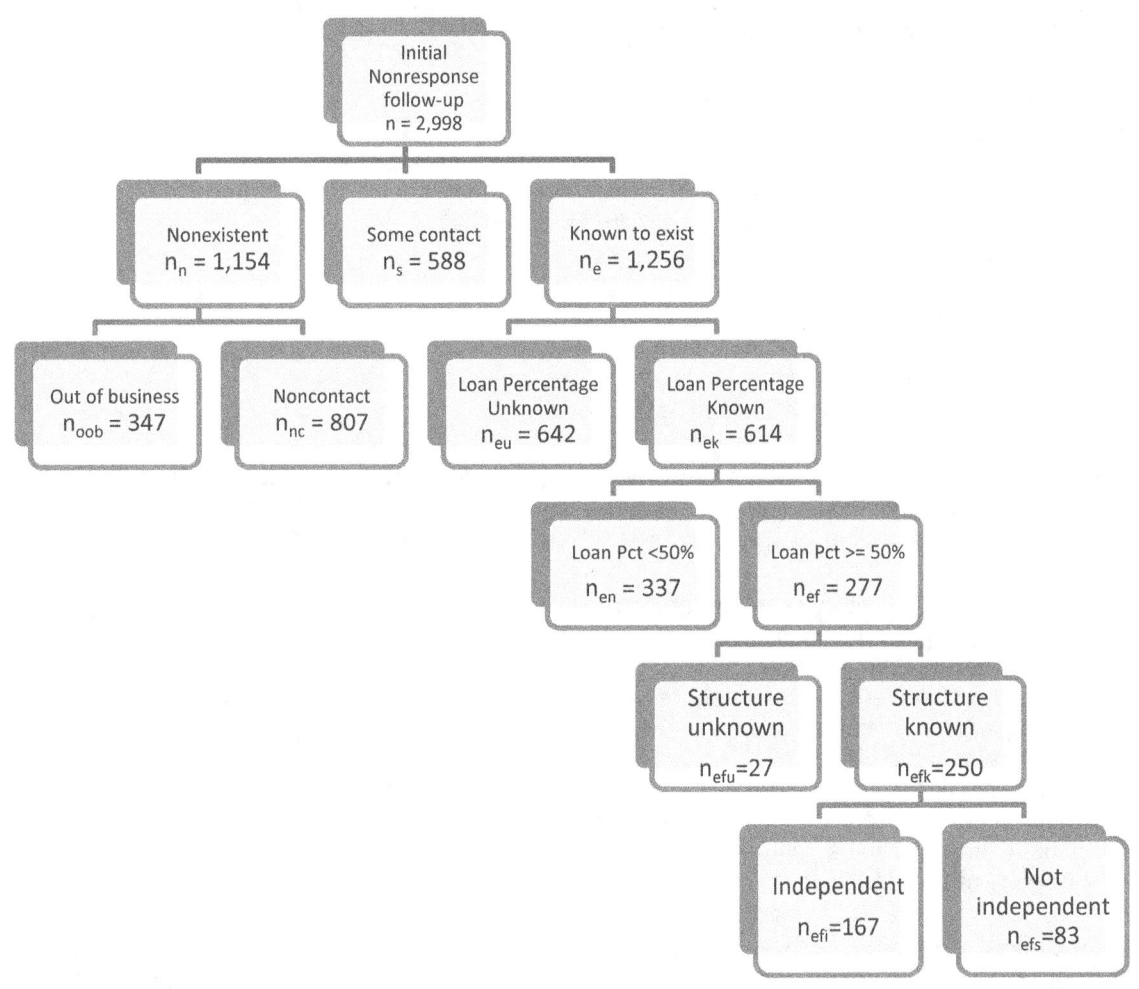

Figure 3: Analysis of follow-up responses[21]

---

[21] Includes largely offsetting minor adjustments to account for known businesses that were not included in the original frame.

Appendix A: Target SIC codes for D&B data

6141 Personal Credit Institutions - Establishments primarily engaged in providing loans to individuals. Also included in this industry are establishments primarily engaged in financing retail sales made on the installment plan and financing automobile loans for individuals.

- Automobile loans (may include automobile insurance)
- Consumer finance companies
- Financing of automobiles, furniture, appliances, personal airplanes,
- Industrial loan "banks", not engaged in deposit banking
- Industrial loan companies, not engaged in deposit banking
- Installment sales finance, other than banks
- Loan companies, small: licensed
- Loan societies, remedial
- Morris plans not engaged in deposit banking
- Mutual benefit associations
- Personal finance companies, small loan: licensed

6153 Short-Term Business Credit Institutions, Except Agricultural - Establishments primarily engaged in extending credit to business enterprises for relatively short periods. Private establishments primarily engaged in extending agricultural credit are classified in Industry 6159.

- Business credit institutions, short-term Credit card service,
- Direct working capital financing
- Factors of commercial paper
- Financing of dealers by motor vehicle manufacturers' organizations
- Installment notes, buying of
- Installment paper dealer
- Mercantile financing
- Purchasers of accounts receivable and commercial paper
- Trust deeds, purchase and sale of
- Working capital financing

6159 Miscellaneous business Credit Institutions - Establishments primarily engaged in furnishing intermediate or long-term general and industrial credit, including the finance leasing of automobiles, trucks, and machinery and equipment. Included in this industry are private establishments primarily engaged in extending agricultural credit. Federal and federally-sponsored credit agencies primarily engaged in extending agricultural credit are classified in Industry 6111. Establishments primarily engaged in other types of leasing of passenger cars and trucks are classified in Industry Group 751.

- Agricultural loan companies
- Automobile finance leasing
- Credit institutions, agricultural
- Farm mortgage companies
- Finance leasing of equipment and vehicles
- General and industrial loan institutions
- Intermediate investment "banks"
- Investment companies, small business
- Livestock loan companies
- Loan institutions, general and industrial
- Machinery and equipment finance leasing
- Pari-mutuel totalizator equipment finance leasing and maintenance
- Production credit association, agricultural
- Truck finance leasing

Appendix B: Source of Initial List Frame

Initial D&B records	26,641
Less: Non US address	90
All missing values in record	30
The word "Bank" appeared in the name	856
The word "Credit Union" appeared in the name	295
Did not have desired SIC code	392
Bank holding company	10
Branch indicator equals 1	18
Exact duplicate	18
Subsidiary of a bank	17
D&B records	24,915
HMDA records	1,000
2005 CFC records	944
Less: duplicated in D&B or HMDA/CFC records	188
Final disposition of the initial frame	26,671
D&B records	24,803
HMDA records	924
2005 CFC records	944

Appendix C: Clustering Procedure

Clustering rule	Number of clusters	Records
First four words in the company name matched	1,663	4,861
First three words matched any of the names above	NA	170
First three words in the company name matched	547	1,222
Large companies in which the first word matched[22]	47	383
Large companies in which the first two words matched	17	237
Less: duplicates among clusters above	-9	NA
Total Clustered	*2,265*	*6,873*
Total not clustered	NA	18,889
Subtotal	NA	25,762
Identified parent companies added to the list frame	NA	12
Identified parent companies in the list frame	NA	7
Out of scope records	NA	902
Total records	NA	26,683

---

[22] Large companies were defined as companies with widely recognized brand names in the U.S. as a part of their name.

Appendix D: Census forms from 2005 and 2010

FR 3033p
OMB No. 7100-0277
Approval expires December 31, 2008

FINANCE COMPANY QUESTIONNAIRE 2005

If address at the left is incorrect, please correct in the space below.

This report is authorized by law [12 U.S.C. §§225(a), 263, 353-359]. Your voluntary cooperation in submitting this report is needed to make the results comprehensive, accurate and timely.

The Federal Reserve System regards the information provided by each respondent as confidential. If it should be determined subsequently that any information collected on this form must be released, respondents will be notified.

INSTRUCTIONS

Reporting Burden
Public reporting burden for this collection of information is estimated to average 15 minutes per response, including the time to gather and maintain data in the required form and to review instructions and complete the information collection. Send comments regarding this burden estimate or any other aspect of this collection of information, including suggestions for reducing this burden to: Secretary, Board of Governors of the Federal Reserve System, 20th & C Streets, N.W. Washington, D.C. 20551; and to the Office of Management and Budget, Paperwork Reduction Project (7100-0277), Washington, D.C. 20503.

Purpose of Report

The purpose of this questionnaire is to provide basic information on a universe of finance companies from which a sample of companies can be selected to answer the 2005 Survey of Finance Companies. That survey will provide benchmark data to update series on consumer and business credit.

The questionnaire concerns the company listed above. If the company name and/or address is incorrect, please provide the correct information in the space to the right of the address. Please answer as many questions as applicable. Return the questionnaire within ten days in the enclosed postage-paid envelope to Micro Statistics Section, Stop 401, Division of Research and Statistics, Board of Governors of the Federal Reserve System, Washington, D.C. 20551.

Scope of the Report

For purposes of this questionnaire, a finance company is defined as a company (excluding credit unions, savings banks, investment banks, commercial banks, cooperative banks, and savings and loan associations) in which the largest portion of the company's assets are in one or more of the following kinds of receivables:

   a. *Consumer receivables* - receivables arising from retail sales of passenger cars and mobile homes, other consumer goods, such as general merchandise, apparel, furniture and household appliances, and/or from outlays for home improvement loans not secured by real estate. Unsecured personal loans, such as loans for education or to pay for insurance policies; or personal loans secured by collateral, such as insurance policies or autos already paid for, etc.;

   b. *Short- and intermediate-term business receivables including leasing* - loans on commercial accounts receivable, inventory loans, factoring, leasing, retail installment sales (or purchases) of commercial, industrial and farm equipment and commercial vehicles, and wholesale financing of consumer and business goods;

   c. *Liens on real estate* - loans, whatever the purpose, secured by liens on real estate as evidenced by mortgages, deeds of trust, land contracts or other instruments;

1. If the above company no longer exists, please give reason:
   () a.   Out of business, in liquidation or in bankruptcy
   () b.   Sold to another firm (Please give name and address of other firm)
         Company name _____
         Street address _____
         City, state, zip code _____
   () c.   Other (specify) _____

DO NOT COMPLETE QUESTIONS 2 THROUGH 5 IF COMPANY NO LONGER EXISTS

2. Is the above named company a finance company as defined above?
   () No   () Yes

3. Does the company specialize in only one of the kind of receivables included in the definition above?
   () No   () a.   Consumer receivables
   () Yes (Check only your specialty at right)   () b.   Short- and intermediate-term business receivables
                                                       (including leases)
                                                 () c.   Liens on real estate

4. How large are the company's total assets?
   () a.   Less than $1 million   () d.   At least $100 million, but less than $1 billion
   () b.   At least $1 million, but less than $10 million   () e.   At least $1 billion, but less than $3 billion
   () c.   At least $10 million, but less than $100 million   () f.   At least $3 billion, but less than $20 billion
                                                     () g. $20 billion or more

5. If the above company is a branch of a finance company or a subsidiary of another company, please provide the following information:
Name of parent or home office _____
Street address _____
City, state, zip code _____
Parent of home office is:
   () a.   Finance company (as defined above)   () d.   Retailer
   () b.   Bank   () e.   Manufacturer
   () c.   Bank holding company   () f.   Other (specify) _____

FR 3033p- XXXXXXXXX
OMB No. 7100-0277
Approval Expires April 2013

2010 CENSUS OF FINANCE COMPANIES

NAME
POSITION
NAME OF COMPANY
STREET ADDRESS
CITY, STATE ZIP

START HERE

Please return the form within 15 days of receipt.

Complete the census online at:
www.federalreserve.gov/financecocensus/

    Log on ID:
    XXXXXXXXX
    Your unique online pass code:
    XXXXXXXXX

OR, if you prefer

Mail your completed form to:
    Board of Governors of the
    Federal Reserve System
    Micro Statistics Section, stop 186
    20th and C Streets NW
    Washington, DC 20551

Need help or have questions?

Visit:
www.federalreserve.gov/financecocensus/

Email:
rsma-financecocensus@frb.gov

Call toll-free to leave a message:
1-866-359-6619

The Federal Reserve is collecting information:

- on companies that supply credit or lease financing to households or businesses

- to provide the Federal Reserve with a baseline picture of the providers of credit in the U.S. economy.

Your response is important and your answers will be kept CONFIDENTIAL.

Please answer as many questions as applicable using data as of March 31, 2010.

Legal authorization: This information collection is authorized by law [12 U.S.C. §§225(a), 263, 353-359]. Although participation is voluntary, your company is an important part of this effort and your assistance is greatly appreciated.

Respondent burden: We expect it will take you about 20 minutes to respond to this census, including the time required to review the instructions, gather the data, and complete the census. If you have comments about the time and effort required for you to respond, how we might reduce this time and effort, or any other aspect of this collection of information, please send to:

    Secretary
    Board of Governors of the Federal Reserve System
    20th & C Streets NW, Washington, DC 20551

    and to:

    Office of Management and Budget
    Paperwork Reduction Project (7100-0277)
    Washington, DC 20503

FR 3033p- XXXXXXXX

2010 CENSUS OF FINANCE COMPANIES

1. Is the company still in business?

   ☐ Yes *(please go to question 2)*
   ☐ No *(check reason below)*

   ☐ Sold to another company *(please print name and address of other company)*

   Company name

   Street address

   City   State   Zip code

   ☐ No longer in operation
   ☐ Other *(please specify)*

If the company is no longer in business, please go to question 10.

2. How large were the company's total assets as of March 31, 2010? Please include only assets in the US, Puerto Rico, or US territories and possessions.

   ☐ Less than $1 million   ☐ $1 billion - less than $3 billion
   ☐ $1 million - less than $10 million   ☐ $3 billion - less than $20 billion
   ☐ $10 million - less than $100 million   ☐ $20 billion or more
   ☐ $100 million - less than $1 billion

3. Loans and leases represent what percentage of total assets?

   ☐ 0% - 24%   ☐ 50% - 74%
   ☐ 25% - 49%   ☐ 75% - 100%

4. Which of the following make up 50 percent or more of the company's loans and leases?

   ☐ Business credit
   ☐ Consumer credit
   ☐ Liens on real estate
   ☐ No single type represents 50 percent or more of total loans and leases

Business loans and leases *refers to outstanding balances on loans or leases not secured by real estate that are made to sole proprietorships, partnerships, corporations or other business enterprises for commercial, industrial, or agricultural purposes;*
Consumer loans and leases *refers to outstanding balances on loans or leases not secured by real estate that are made to households for household, family, and other personal expenditures; and*
Liens on real estate *refers to outstanding balances on loans or leases secured by real estate that are made to any person or business for any purpose.*

OMB No. 7100-0277
Approval expires April 2013

Please continue to final page →

5. Is the company licensed by a state or federal authority as a:

☐ Commercial bank, cooperative bank, credit union, savings bank, or savings and loan association

☐ Bank holding company

☐ None of the above

6. Is the company a branch or subsidiary of another company?

☐ Yes *(please complete questions 7-10)*   ☐ No *(please skip to question 10)*

7. Please print the following information:

Name of parent company

Street address

City   State   Zip code

8. Do loans or leases typically make up 50 percent or more of your parent company's total assets?

☐ Yes   ☐ No   ☐ Do not know

9. Is your parent company licensed by a state or federal authority as a:

☐ Commercial bank, cooperative bank, credit union, savings bank, or savings and loan association

☐ Bank holding company

☐ None of the above

10. Please provide us with your current contact information.

Your name

Phone   Ext.

Email

If the company name/address on the cover page was incorrect, please correct below.

Thank you for completing the 2010 Census of Finance Companies.

OMB No. 7100-0277
Approval expires April 2013

Appendix E: Editing responses to the CFC

In order to minimize the effects of response error and error in the scanning of paper questionnaires, the data were subjected to a thorough review. Because the CFC is effectively a screening device designed to determine which companies qualify as finance companies, the review focused on editing the most important questions needed to make this determination. In the end, we made the determination based on six questions on the CFC, resulting in a six-stage editing process. Due to resource limitations, we designed the review so that if at the end of an editing stage, a company was determined to be out of scope, it was not included in the next editing stage.[23] In stage one, we reviewed whether the company was still in business (company status). In stage two, we reviewed the percent of assets in loans and lease receivables for companies whose company status was "in business." In stage three, we reviewed the company type for the respondents that met the definition of a financial institution (more than 50 percent of assets in loans and leases). In stage four, we reviewed the company's corporate structure for respondents identified as a finance company (not a depository or a bank holding company). In stage five, we reviewed the company's parent loan and lease concentration for finance companies that we identified as a subsidiary of another company. Finally, in stage 6, we reviewed the parent company type for companies that were the subsidiaries of financial institutions.

Appendix F: Item nonresponse imputation

Our goal in the CFC is not only to estimate the total number of finance companies in the United States, but also to estimate the number of finance companies by size of company and lending specialty. The final step before estimating the universe of finance companies by size and specialty was to address the issue of nonresponse in one or more of these items. The item nonresponse rate for both variables was about 3 percent of all the entities that were independent finance companies. Generally, if the respondent answered the asset size question, they also answered the lending specialty question: where asset size information was available, the item nonresponse rate for specialty was only one-half percent.

We used a type of randomized hot deck multiple imputation to impute missing size and specialty variables. This imputation method involves creating classes of respondents based on data that are

---

[23] The editing process was repeated twice in case edits at later stages of the process might affect the outcome of earlier stages.

available for all respondents and randomly matching a "donor" respondent who has complete size and specialty data with a "recipient" respondent who has incomplete size and specialty data. To enable estimation of the uncertainty surrounding this imputation, the process was repeated five times (Rubin, 1987). Comparison of the five imputation sets concluded that there was only slight difference among them. For simplicity, one of the imputation sets was then randomly chosen as the final estimate.

www.ingramcontent.com/pod-product-compliance
Lightning Source LLC
Chambersburg PA
CBHW080640290526
45790CB00007B/3149